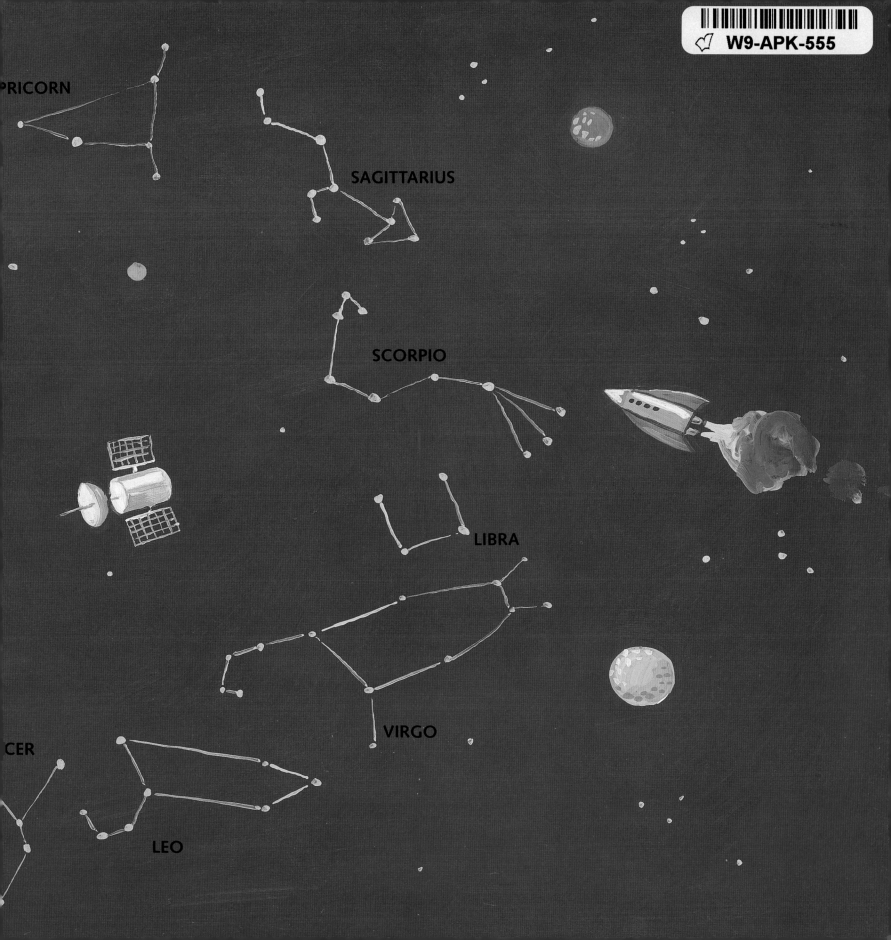

For my parents (both Cancer), who watch over me.
C.N.

INTRODUCTION

The sky above us is full of stars. As they criss-cross the heavens, they change what the sky looks like. The Sun, the Moon, and the Planets dance among these stars, and the pattern of this dance in the sky is called the Zodiac. The Zodiac is divided into twelve Star Signs and, depending on your birthday, one of these Signs is yours – do you know which one? For a long, long time, people have believed that the position of the stars at our birth influences what we are like and what happens to us.

Each Sign is ruled by a Planet. The ruling Planet represents the specific kind of energy the Sign will give off. Each Sign also belongs to one of four Elements: Fire 🔥, Air ♎, Earth △, or Water ≋. Leo, Aries, and Sagittarius are Fire Signs, full of energy. Aquarius, Gemini, and Libra are Air Signs, cool and thoughtful. Capricorn, Taurus, and Virgo are Earth Signs, practical and level-headed. Cancer, Pisces, and Scorpio are Water Signs, emotional and caring.

This book, *Star Signs*, illustrates each Sign and can help you start learning about the Zodiac. The more time you spend studying the Zodiac, the more you can learn about yourself, your family, and your friends. You may notice that people who are born under the same Sign often can be very alike. See if you can recognize yourself in these pages!

Published by Turner Publishing, Inc.
A Subsidiary of Turner Broadcasting System, Inc.
1050 Techwood Drive, N.W.
Atlanta, Georgia 30318

First Edition 10 9 8 7 6 5 4 3 2 1
Hardcover ISBN 1–57036–011–1
Library of Congress Card Catalog Number: 93–61866

An Albion Book

Conceived, designed, and produced by
The Albion Press Ltd, Spring Hill, Idbury,
Oxfordshire OX7 6RU, England

Text copyright © 1994 Caroline Ness
Illustrations copyright © 1994 Emily Bolam
Volume copyright © 1994 The Albion Press Ltd

Project Manager: Jane Lahr
Editor: Robin Aigner
Art Director: Vickey Bolling

Distributed by Andrews and McMeel
A Universal Press Syndicate Company
4900 Main Street
Kansas City, Missouri 64112

ASHBROOK

STAR SIGNS

EMILY BOLAM ♈ CAROLINE NESS

Turner Publishing, Inc.

ATLANTA

ARIES THE DAREDEVIL

Aries, the ram, is the trailblazer of our zodiac. He is ruled by Mars, the planet of energy and courage, so he likes to lead the parade. Aries gets straight to the heart of a problem.

Aries is always ready for action. Because he is a daredevil, he often takes risks. Aries likes to win, and when he wants something badly, he doesn't like to wait!

Aries knows what he wants and does not let anyone hold him back. When he is angry, he often speaks before he thinks, so sometimes he can hurt the feelings of others.

Aries is popular and makes friends easily and eagerly. He accepts people as they are.
Best friends: Leos and Sagittarians.
Also good friends: Aquarians and Geminis.

TAURUS THE PLEASURE-SEEKE

Taurus, the bull, is a gentle giant. He is good-natured and slow to anger, but if you wave a red flag in front of his face, this stubborn bull may charge!

Taurus is reliable, businesslike, and steady. He is always careful and thinks before he acts. He has common sense and takes his time before coming to a decision.

Taurus is ruled by Venus, the planet of art and music, and loves all the best things in life. He'll surround himself with luxury and beauty, and then lie back and enjoy them.

Taurus is a faithful friend. He is loving and protective. Best friends: Capricorns and Virgos. Other good friends: Cancers and Pisceans.

GEMINI THE DYNAMIC DUO

The twins are ruled by the planet Mercury, so they are full of mischief and have busy imaginations. Geminis are usually charming, talented, and fun to be with.

Clever and curious, Geminis are always eager to learn, but sometimes they get bored and need new ideas and variety in their lives. In crowds, they like to be the entertainers.

 **SIGN: GEMINI**  **PLANET: MERCURY** **ELEMENT: AIR** 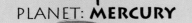 **22ND MAY – 21ST JUNE**

Geminis do not like to feel trapped, so they dance their way out of trouble with energy and style. Geminis are smart and creative and will usually land on their feet.

Outgoing, talkative, and funny, Geminis are always good company and make many friends. Best friends: Aquarians and Librans. Also good friends: Arians and Leos.

CANCER THE NEST BUILDER

Cancer, the crab, loves her home. She will have a strong sense of duty to her family all through her life. But sometimes she can be too protective and emotional with those she loves.

The crab is a mysterious and imaginative creature. Ruled by the Moon, she hides her feelings and can be moody. One minute she may seem gloomy, but the next she can be on top of the world.

In the face of problems, Cancer's insight and quick thinking will see her through. Cancer likes to feel needed and will rush to defend anyone weaker than herself.

Cancer has a caring and sensitive nature — she will be your friend for life. Best friends: Pisceans and Scorpios. Other good friends: Taureans and Virgos.

LEO THE SUN KING

Leo, the lion, is the "star" of stars in our zodiac. Always the leader, Leo is bold and full of energy. He thinks and acts big, and always believes that he knows best.

This lion is larger than life. A big-hearted and natural showman, Leo will roar with frustration if he isn't the center of attention. He can be a show-off and a bully.

Leo never gives up, even when he's taken on far too much. He walks on the sunny side of the street. Witty and always entertaining, Leo makes great company.

Ruled by the Sun, Leo is bright, warm, and generous. He is a loyal companion. Best friends: Arians and Sagittarians. Other good friends: Librans and Geminis.

VIRGO THE EARTH MOTHER

Virgo, the maiden, is a child of nature, so she loves to be outdoors. She is ruled by Mercury, the planet of intelligence. Hard-working and level-headed, Virgo wants the best for herself and others.

Virgo enjoys keeping herself busy and being helpful. She likes mending things and tries to make sure that everything is perfect. But with so much to do, she can worry too much.

Virgo likes to take care of people and problems. She does not seek praise, but gets the job done. Behind her seriousness and shyness, she hides a warm heart.

Virgo is kind, loyal, and helpful; she puts her friends' interests before her own. Best friends: Capricorns and Taureans. Other good friends: Cancers and Scorpios.

LIBRA THE DIPLOMAT

Libra's sign is the scales, which stand for balance and harmony. She is ruled by Venus, the planet of love and art. A talented speaker with a sense of fair play, Libra is the peacemaker of the zodiac.

She can see all sides of a problem, and this can make Libra hesitate when making decisions. She hates to argue and would rather make peace than lose a friend.

SIGN: **LIBRA**   PLANET: **VENUS**   ELEMENT: **AIR**   24TH SEPTEMBER-23RD OCTOBER

Libra won't be pushed or rushed into anything. Relaxed, friendly, and eager to please, she is a good pal. She needs to have close friendships and doesn't like to be alone.

A real romantic, Libra is in love with love. Best friends: Aquarians and Geminis. Other good friends: Leos and Sagittarians.

SCORPIO THE DETECTIVE

Scorpio, the scorpion, is the private eye of our zodiac. He is ruled by Pluto, the planet of great mysteries. He has a sharp mind and will dig deep to discover hidden secrets.

Scorpio is an intense person, so others are often attracted to him. He has a lot of self-confidence and willpower. Watch out: If angered, he can have a bad temper!

One of the most powerful signs in the zodiac, he does things all the way or not at all. He often plays the hero, but can be very sensitive and easily hurt.

Scorpio chooses friends carefully and stands by them through thick and thin. Best friends: Cancers and Pisceans. Other good friends: Capricorns and Virgos.

SAGITTARIUS THE ADVENTURE

Sagittarius, the archer, is the explorer of the zodiac. He is ruled by Jupiter, the planet of growth of the mind. A teacher as well as a student, he likes to travel to explore new horizons.

Life for Sagittarius is a voyage of discovery. Capable, energetic, and daring, he may get bored without new challenges. He likes to take risks, but can be a little reckless.

N: **SAGITTARIUS** PLANET: **JUPITER** ELEMENT: **FIRE**

23ʳᵈ NOVEMBER – 21ˢᵀ DECEMBER

Honest, trustworthy, and wise, Sagittarius is always an optimist. Independent, he needs plenty of space to breathe and may get restless if others try to tie him down.

Sagittarius is an outgoing person and a good friend with a gentle and forgiving nature. Best friends: Arians and Leos. Other good friends: Aquarians and Librans.

CAPRICORN THE CONQUERO

Capricorn, the goat, is ruled by Saturn, the planet of duty. He is as steady as a rock. Determined and reliable, he will win against all odds. However, his soft-spoken manner may hide a fighting spirit.

Capricorn appears organized and calm, but underneath there lurks a zany sense of humor. He sets high standards, and wants to succeed no mat how long it takes! He can achieve great things.

Capricorn is businesslike and sensible – he always tries to do the right thing. He expects others to work as hard as he does, so he can seem demanding, but he usually gets good results.

Capricorn is shy about showing his feelings, but he is true and loyal to a friend in need. Best friends: Taureans and Virgos. Other good friends: Pisceans and Scorpios.

AQUARIUS THE FREE SPIRIT

Aquarius, the water-bearer, is an inventor and a rebel. Ruled by Uranus, the planet of surprise, Aquarius loves the unusual or unexpected. She can be quite full of surprises herself!

Independent and freethinking, Aquarius likes to do things in her own way. She can be stubborn and sometimes appears lost in thought, but she is also fair and truthful.

Aquarius is very friendly and cares deeply for others. Although she may seem happiest in a group of people, she leads a private life and likes to spend time alone.

It may be hard to get close to Aquarius, but once she is a friend, she is kind, devoted, and loyal. Best friends: Geminis and Librans. Other good friends: Arians and Sagittarians.

PISCES THE HEALER

Pisces, the fish, is ruled by Neptune, the planet of fantasy and mystery. Pisces cares more about feelings than facts. He could daydream his life away.

Pisces is blessed with a vivid and colorful imagination and is often highly creative. He is always open to new ideas, but if not careful, he can easily be tricked.

GN: **PISCES** PLANET: **NEPTUNE** ELEMENT: **WATER** 20ᵀᴴ FEBRUARY – 20ᵀᴴ MARCH

Comforting, understanding, and tender, Pisces s a natural healer. Sometimes he is so busy taking care of others that he forgets about himself.

Pisces is everyone's favorite because he is so carefree, sensitive, and loving. Best friends: Scorpios and Cancers. Other good friends: Capricorns and Taureans.

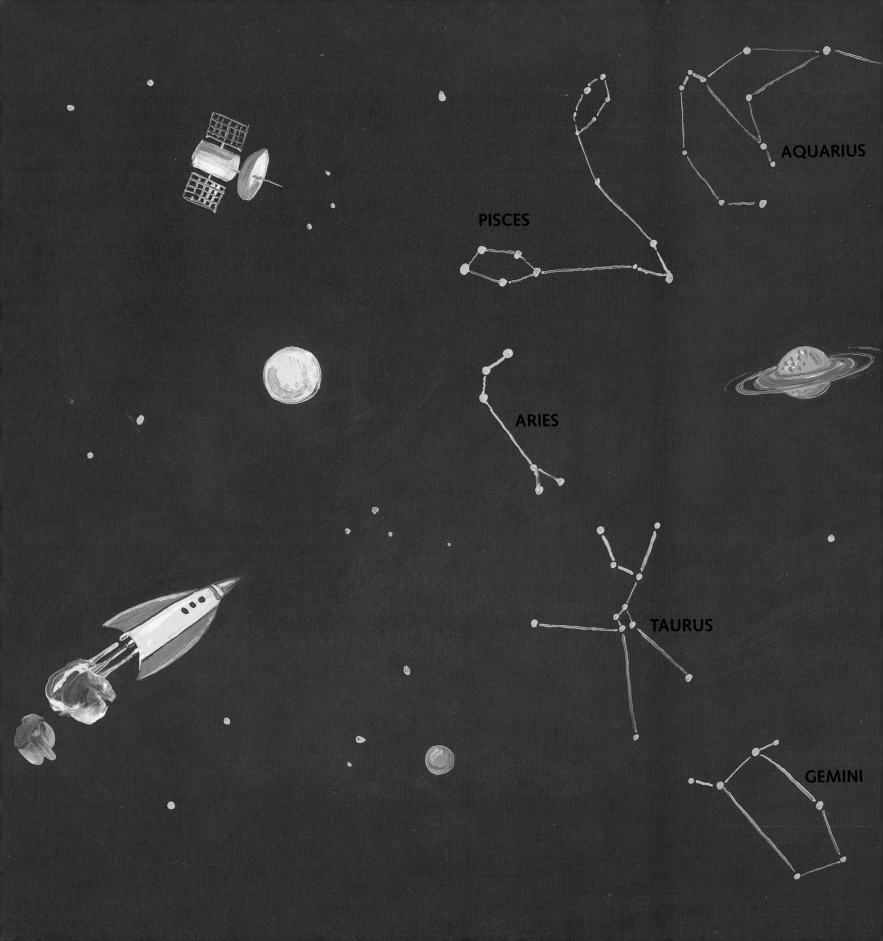